TO THE EXTREME

BMX Racing

by Angie Peterson Kaelberer

Reading Consultant:
Barbara J. Fox
Reading Specialist
North Carolina State University

Capstone
press

Mankato, Minnesota

Blazers is published by Capstone Press,
151 Good Counsel Drive, P.O. Box 669, Mankato, Minnesota 56002.
www.capstonepress.com

Library of Congress Cataloging-in-Publication Data
Kaelberer, Angie Peterson.
   BMX racing / by Angie Peterson Kaelberer.
   p. cm.—(Blazers. To the extreme)
   Summary: "Describes the sport of BMX racing, including
equipment and safety information"—Provided by publisher.
   Includes bibliographical references and index.
   ISBN 0-7368-4397-3 (hardcover)
   ISBN 0-7368-6174-2 (softcover)
   1. Bicycle motocross—Juvenile literature. I. Title. II. Series.
GV1049.3.K34 2006
796.6'2—dc22   2005001431

Credits

Jason Knudson, set designer; Kate Opseth, book designer; Jo Miller,
   photo researcher; Scott Thoms, photo editor

Photo Credits

Getty Images Inc./Tony Ashby, 26
SportsChrome Inc./Sport the library, 23
TransWorld BMX/Keith Mulligan, cover, 5, 6, 7, 8, 9, 11, 12, 13, 14, 15,
   16–17, 19, 20, 24, 25, 28–29

**Capstone Press thanks Keith Mulligan, Editor/Photographer,
TransWorld BMX magazine, for his assistance with this book.**

1 2 3 4 5 6 10 09 08 07 06 05

Table of Contents

Out of the Gate

The starting gate drops. The BMX racers speed over the first jumps of the track.

The racers pump their pedals fast and hard. Warwick Stevenson pulls to the front of the pack.

BLAZER FACT

BMX is short for bicycle motocross.

Stevenson streaks across the finish line. He wins the main event and the gold medal.

Equipment

Racing bikes are built for speed. Many bike frames are made of a strong, lightweight metal called aluminum.

Frame

Knobby tires grip the dirt tracks.
The bumpy tires keep bikes from
sliding on the track.

BLAZER FACT

The built-up turns of
a BMX track are
called berms.

Knobby tire

Clipless pedal

Clipless pedals hold shoes to
the pedals. Clipless pedals help the
racers ride faster.

BMX Bike Diagram

Knobby tire

Helmet

Number plate

Frame

Clipless pedal

17

Competitions

BMX events have several levels. Winners of the first races move up to the semifinals. Semifinal winners race in the main event.

Pro racers make their living racing. They have sponsors. These companies give the racers money and equipment.

Safety

All BMX racers wear helmets.
The helmets cover much of the
head and face.

Racers protect their bodies with long-sleeved shirts and long pants. The clothes are made of a material that helps racers stay cool.

Pads under their clothes protect riders when they fall. Riders wear pads on their knees, shins, elbows, and wrists.

Racing around a berm!

hyperbicycles.com

hyperbicycles.com

29

Glossary

aluminum (uh-LOO-mi-nuhm)—a strong, lightweight metal used to make racing bikes

berm (BIRM)—a built-up turn or corner on a BMX track

frame (FRAYM)—the body of a bike

pedal (PED-uhl)—a lever on a bicycle that riders push with their feet

semifinals (SEM-ee-fye-nuhls)—races that determine which racers will compete in the main event

sponsor (SPON-sur)—a company or organization that gives a racer equipment or money to race

Read More

Schuette, Sarah L. *Downhill BMX*. To the Extreme. Mankato, Minn.: Capstone Press, 2005.

Vieregger, K. E. *BMX Riding*. X-treme Sports. Edina, Minn.: Abdo, 2003.

Weil, Ann. *BMX Racing*. X-Sports. Mankato, Minn.: Capstone Press, 2005.

Wingate, Brian. *BMX Bicycle Racing: Techniques and Tricks*. Rad Sports. New York: Rosen, 2003.

Internet Sites

FactHound offers a safe, fun way to find Internet sites related to this book. All of the sites on FactHound have been researched by our staff.

Here's how:

1. Visit *www.facthound.com*
2. Type in this special code **0736843973** for age-appropriate sites. Or enter a search word related to this book for a more general search.
3. Click on the **Fetch It** button.

FactHound will fetch the best sites for you!

Index